How an
Ordinary Girl
Finds
Extraordinary
Love

A WISE DOG'S OBSERVATIONS ON THE HOOMAN EXPERIENCE

TAMMIE HOMEYER SHELTON
Assisted by GG, the Wise Dog

ISBN 978-1-0980-2160-3 (paperback)
ISBN 978-1-0980-2625-7 (hardcover)
ISBN 978-1-0980-2161-0 (digital)

Christian Faith Publishing, Inc.
832 Park Avenue
Meadville, PA 16335
www.christianfaithpublishing.com

Printed in the United States of America

To my Tracer,
We're really doin' it, hey buddy?

CONTENTS

ACKNOWLEDGMENTS

Without the encouragement and not-so-gentle-pushing of my soul mate and laugh-mate, my husband, this book would have never happened. Thank you, Tracy. The world is a much better place because you were in it. I love you.

Desi and Alyssa, the world needs more of what we have. Someday we will start a movement through chick-and-chicken lunches.

Brad, thank you for allowing me to be your other mom. Your dad sure loved you, and so do I.

My grandchildren are genuine examples of extraordinary love—how to give it and how to receive it. You each taught me easily as much as I have taught you. Nonnie loves you very much—extraordinarily!

My brothers, you taught me to be tough but still let me be the princess of the family. I am grateful for all the life lessons we learned as we grew up together.

Cindy and Terri, thank you for sharing your brother with me. You are my sisters—gained through marriage but gifted by God.

I am so grateful for the many friends, mentors, and family members who taught me how to appreciate God's love and his gifts. You know who you are.

Bethany, my dear other mom, thank you for introducing me to the concept that it doesn't matter how you found yourself in a family. Whether by birth, adoption, marriage, divorce, or a myriad other ways—however you got here—you are still family.

Mom, I miss you. You would have been proud of this book even though you didn't really like GG (or any dog) very much. Thank you for believing I could do no wrong and for teaching me to know better.

Daddy, I love you. Thank you for raising me to have a love of and trust in our Lord. You provided the strong foundation that led to my becoming a strong, faithful, happy woman.

INTRODUCTION

I Am a Dog

My name is GG. And you might as well know it up front—I am a dog. I am a big black part-lab, part-hound rescue mutt. Mom says I am majestic and sophisticated, like a Lab. It makes sense because she is always trying to build up my self-esteem by loving on me. Dad, on the other hand, says I am a *hound* dawg. His assessment might have something to do with my usually droopy red eyes and the drool that continually covers, well, everything around me. His nickname for me may be his way of putting a limit on my self-esteem. I'm okay with it all. I just think those are how they show love. Mom wants me to feel important, beautiful, and loved, and Dad wants me to stay humble. (Truth be told, he spoils me more than Mom does). They have different parenting styles, but the situation somehow works. Maybe this is what Mom means when she says kids need mother *and* father figures in their lives.

I earned my name when I somehow managed to fall *up* the stairs on the day I was adopted. In my defense, I was only ten months old, and my body had not quite grown into my big paws or my huge ears. I also have an extremely long tail, which is necessary to counterbalance the ears, and it possibly tripped me. I do have to say now, though, that God is so smart to give those of us with huge ears a big, giant tail to counterbalance them. Who else would think of doing that? On top of the ear and tail challenges, I had never, in my life, seen open stairs, so the whole day was a challenge. All I do know is I not so gracefully fell *up* instead of *down* the stairs. (Just for the record, I am also smart and a quick learner, and from that moment

9

on, I playfully prance *down* those stairs and gracefully glide *up* the ramp.) After that slightly embarrassing episode, my parents named me GG, which is short for Gangly Girl. Sometimes they change it to Goofy Girl or Goober Girl, depending on the circumstances. Often I am God's Girl when I am *really* sweet and good, and heck, now I think GG could mean Glider Girl. (Because I glide up the ramp—get it?) Sometimes they call me Pretty Girl (which I do not understand because my name isn't PG). The reality is that I answer to a lot of names. But now, just for the record, I am pretty sure they have never called me Graceful Girl, and I can understand why. Whatever they call me, I always feel the love in their voices, and I can see it in their faces. But so you don't get confused, I will stick with GG for the purposes of this book.

Although an authentic southern girl never reveals her *true* age, I will admit that I am nine-ish years old as I write this, and I have seen a lot of this round planet that revolves around me. I have gratefully and excitedly observed so much hope in our world yet sadly also witnessed more than my share of despair. This particular narrative is mostly about my observations on love. You will read about a lot of hope and will even find a hint of despair in my story, but you will also notice that it focuses on love; any despair you read here will circle around and find its way back to love. What I have experienced and observed has opened my heart to a truly beautiful universe. My world is full of many different types of love, and love has led to the chapters of this book. You might think it is about romantic love, and there certainly is a chapter that talks about the love of a lover, but most of this book talks about other types of love, including God's love, the love of nature, the love of animals, and others. After all, if we have love—a whole lot of it and a whole lot of types of it—this world can become an amazing place to live in—even with negative emotional turmoil or traumatic and dramatic events. I am living proof of this fact, and so are Mom and Dad.

PROLOGUE

How This Book Came to Be: What Is Extraordinary Love?

I started this book in a hotel room because Mom, Dad, and I were displaced due to Hurricane Harvey, which hit the Texas Gulf Coast in August 2017. You might have heard about it; Harvey was a big one! Hurricanes can wreak havoc on a community and a family, as I found out firsthand. Yet life had been quite crazy and a bit stressful at our Rockport, Texas, home even before Harvey hit. My hound-dog eyes fill with red streaks when I am stressed or tired, and my eyes had a lot of streaks lately. (Okay, Dad, maybe I really am a hound dawg and not a majestic Lab.)

I find it extremely weird and so very sad that three of us evacuated because of the hurricane but only two of us returned to a somewhat-normal life at home. Yet even the sad story you will read about later has a whole lot of love in it, and I bet it will make you smile more than it will make you cry. I promise that more details will be included throughout my story. But I am getting ahead of myself, and there is so much more to this story than a family of three turning into a family of two.

My narrative chronicles more than forty years of love. Obviously, I am not that old, but I trust that my mom was being honest when she shared her memories with me. Most of the observations are mine, but some are hers, some are Dad's, and some stories come from others. But they are all delivered from my perspective, and all of them will hold true to my perspective about love: love is good, love is abundant, and love is truly extraordinary.

How Did This Title Come to Life?

I knew you would ask that! Mom has been talking about writing a book with this title since before I was born and even before she met Dad. She says her life has been so full of love and she is bursting to share it. Many people who know Mom agree that her story should be shared and have also encouraged her to write this book. She just could not decide how to organize it on paper and never made the time to sit and write. I was so frustrated; I wanted her to write, but she just procrastinated! However, she already started the chapters and outline. Don't tell her this, please—I stole her idea and am presenting it as mine. I must admit that the stories of love mostly come from what she has experienced in her life, so I will give her at least a little of the credit for the story line.

Goodness knows I have more time than Mom does. Well, sort of. In order to find the time to write, I had to give up a nap or two, and my lizard hunting had to be postponed. Oh, and there's the obligatory neighborhood watch I had to squeeze in between paragraphs. I cannot tell you how many mailmen tried to sneak by as I wrote down these words! I also have to share that it is extremely difficult to type with paws and no opposable thumbs, so it takes me a bit longer than a hooman to get this manuscript on paper. Despite my obstacles, I trust you will find this book worth reading. I think it is good enough for *you* to give up a nap or two to finish it.

You probably figured out by now that I am not a doctor or a psychologist and this is not a self-help book. Heh, I just had to say that. Anyway, this narrative is not meant to fix anyone or anything. It is just my story; it is simply a journal about a dog and her observations on love and life. Even though I cannot fix anything or anyone, I do hope my tale (pun intended, ha-ha) inspires you to find and develop your own extraordinary loves and to write your own story. And when you do, I hope you will share it with me.

How to Read This Book

Before we get started, I want to share a little tidbit on how the book is arranged. It is not written in chronological order; rather, each chapter covers a different love topic. So while it is meant to be read from beginning to end, it was not written that way. So if a particular chapter appeals to you, go ahead and read it first. You might come across a spoiler or two, but you also might find exactly what you need at the time. So however you choose to read my observations on love, please enjoy this book in the spirit in which it is intended—to share love and gratitude from an ordinary girl who managed to find extraordinary love.

CHAPTER 1

Love of God / Love of Giving (Together Because They Belong Together)

Expressing Ultimate Love

Mom says the ultimate way to love someone is to put that person's needs before your own. I mostly get it; she and Dad take pretty good care of me, and I can tell that they always put me first! And our love is reciprocal; I am convinced that they hung the moon, and I have no problem with putting them first—well, except for when I need to eat or go to the potty or get attention (like a butt scratch and an ear rub [not necessarily at the same time]) or when I want a walk. Hmm... okay, fine. Maybe I do not really understand how to put someone else first. I am a dog, after all. But I do understand that they know how. And I know without a doubt that God definitely knows too.

We have always been churchgoers, but for Mom and Dad, church and God and worship extend much further than a building or even a religion. They believe God sent his son, Jesus, to save us (I think it is "us"—surely I am included!), and goodness, this is one definitive example of putting others before yourself. Can you imagine? God had only one son, and he sacrificed him to save a world that is pretty messed up. If this is not putting someone else first, I don't know what is.

Mom and Dad live their faith every day even though they go to church just on Sundays. They are pretty respectful of what others believe, but they are also steadfast in their own beliefs. Their faith in God and his ultimate sacrifice is the foundation of so much of their love for each other and for their love of everything else that has been made a chapter in this book.

They say they learned how to treat each other and to put each other's needs ahead of their own by learning how to put God first in their marriage. They learned about love from God. In fact, Mom said we could write a whole book on God's love, and maybe I will someday. But for now, many people have already done that, and most of them know a whole lot more about God than I do. Yet I knew it was important to start this book with Mom and Dad's love of God and his love for them. In all my time in this world, I just haven't seen any example of greater love.

God and Giving Money

When it comes to love of God, how do you demonstrate it? How can you feel it? How do you show love to someone who you cannot physically hug? I think a lot of people and dogs attempt to figure that out every day. I know I totally embrace the sunshine, the occasional romp in the water, and of course, the lizard hunting. Enjoying nature is how I demonstrate my feelings for God's love. I get to experience the best of his world! I will share more about this in the nature chapter. You can look forward to reading more of my extraordinary love secrets then.

One way to demonstrate God's love or to give him a hug is to donate money. The Bible calls for each of us to donate 10 percent of our income. Mom and Dad strive to reach that goal and then some. I have to admit, Mom is a little bit more giving than Dad is. Dad says Mom will write a check to anyone! Dad has a generous, giving heart, yet he is much more cautious about whom he gives to and *when* he gives. Dad believes you should give *after* you make money, and Mom is adamant that you should give *before* you make money. Mom tends to challenge Dad financially as she is certain that it is the right thing to do in the end, and he usually doesn't fight her assertions. But there are definitely times when Dad makes more sense and Mom has to agree. While Dad is a little more guarded and a lot more practical, Mom is a little more carefree with the funds. Isn't that the balance for which we all strive? Mom *and* Dad? Yin *and* yang? I do need to clarify that Mom will always acquiesce to Dad when he stresses his opinion. They just have a great amount of respect for each other. I love to watch them interact about money; it is another way I can see how much they love and admire each other.

But through it all, I have to laugh because their giving styles mirror the different ways they treat me and exemplify the reason Mom says we need mother *and* father figures in our lives. They differ on *what* and *when* to give, but they always agree on *how* to give—freely and with gratitude and with hearts full of love. The bottom line is that they are pretty stinkin' awesome with their giving—mainly because it is always done in God's name and with appreciation for all he has given to them.

I do not totally understand how all of this works. But I do know it *does* work. And I know another little side story that I just have to share. When Dad and Mom decided to marry, their pastor instructed them to discuss their finances before the wedding. They shared their incomes, budgets, and financial goals. Dad finally admitted to Mom that he didn't understand; the numbers in her budget just didn't add up, and he didn't get the math. How weird is that? Mom is a spreadsheet/accounting queen, and the math didn't work? But her answer to him was (and still is) "I know it doesn't work. But God works. I write the check to him first, and he takes care of everything else." Her budget was and still is a faith-based budget. To this day, she still writes the first check to God—before she pays any other bills. She also donates money to other worthy charities whether they fit in her budget or not. And I'm here to tell you, whether you understand it or not, it works.

Challenges and Faith

I hope I have not implied that Mom and Dad have never seen financial hardship or other types of challenge; trust me, they have. They have seen medical challenges, deaths of loved ones, financial challenges (including bankruptcy), and just plain old "life is not fair" bologna. But somehow they have always been able to put someone else's needs in front of their own, and that simple act made their own personal challenges a little less noticeable. They have always had enough—enough food, enough money, and always enough love. And in spite of life's challenges, they have always had faith—even when the obstacles were so great they could not see the road ahead of them. But they took the next step in faith, knowing God was leading them. And I can guarantee that because of this faith, life is good no matter what is happening around them. I see it with Mom and Dad and with others.

Whether you give time or money—whether it be to the church or to a not-for-profit entity or to some other greater good, it is true. When you learn to put others before yourself, when you focus on giving instead of getting, and when you quit keeping score, you receive more, and you end up happier.

Go figure. Even I like that math.

Regardless of what they say behind closed doors and regardless of the outcome, I am confident Mom and Dad are convinced that giving is just the right thing to do. They don't give because they get back tenfold. And, dare I say it, they don't need all the money they make anyway. It is a weird juxtaposition; you get more because you give more. I don't understand any of it, but I do know they are very generous with their money. I heard them say it isn't their money to begin with; it is God's. So they get to live on 90 percent of God's money and only have to give away 10 percent. When you look at it from that perspective, it just makes sense—if you are a logical kind of dog or person.

Mom says her goal is to eventually give away 50 percent of her income, and she was almost there when Dad got sick. She took a few steps backward when she resigned from her full-time job to spend more quality time with Dad. But I have a feeling that she will eventually reach that 50 percent goal, and knowing my Mom, it won't take her long.

God and Giving Time

Another way to demonstrate God's love or to put someone else before yourself is to donate your time. I like to donate my time to the kids. I encourage them to walk me and feed me and play with me, and we all benefit. This is the crazy thing I have learned about giving—you get so much more than you give!

Mom and Dad have donated their time for as long as I have known them and long before. They individually volunteered their time even before they met each other. Dad was very big in civic organizations like the Rotary Club. He is a Paul Harris Fellow, which is a really big deal! He also was the president of his local chamber of commerce long before he met Mom. He has given many hours to multiple chambers of commerce and is especially drawn to their leadership programs. Mom is a recipient of the American Institute for Public Service's Jefferson Award, which was given to her for her volunteerism in the disabled community.

Mom and Dad both volunteer at church too; it is very important to them. From ushering to reading the Bible lessons to teaching Sunday school, they have given their time and talent in many different ways throughout the years. But they found their true calling in working with children and adults with special needs.

Special Olympics

They first discovered this calling by volunteering with Special Olympics. Have you ever watched one of their Olympic meets? Or helped with one? Children and adults with special needs bowl, swim, run in all kinds of track events, and compete in many other Olympic-type events. It is such an amazing organization. Mom and Dad helped with their bowling and track meets and donated money to them too. Their favorite volunteer role was being official finish-line huggers! If you want to volunteer and receive a big, giant benefit, go to them! There is definitely a team in your area. www.specialolympics.org

Eels on Wheels

The Eels are a scuba diving club. They teach people with disabilities how to scuba dive and then travel with them to Caribbean locations. Wow. Close your eyes and try to process this. I am a dog. I trust my parents completely. Yet I cannot imagine them putting scuba equipment and a mask on me, telling me everything is okay, and then throwing me off a boat so I can explore an underwater world—no matter how wonderful that world might be! Yet it is exactly what they do with some of their friends with disabilities, which include people with paraplegia or quadriplegia, people who are blind, and people with many other disabilities. I am sure you are shaking your head right now and may feel a bit horrified, so I figure I had better clarify things; they do not literally *throw* them off the boat. Nonetheless, I suspect it surely feels that way to the diver. In reality, every person is trained well, and you will find many wonderful success stories on their website. Please check it out! Needless to say, the Eels on Wheels is an amazing, unique organization. Mom and Dad began volunteering for them in the year 2000—long before I was born. The underwater world is breathtakingly beautiful. (You will read more details about that world soon enough!) Introducing that world to people with disabilities makes my parents pretty darned happy. They leave me behind when they travel to exotic countries, but it still makes me happy. I get to go to Grandma and Grandpa's house most of the time. I have so much fun! But don't tell Mom and Dad because I like to make them think I sulk the whole time. www.eels.org

Camp Aranzazu

Second only to being on or in the water, Mom and Dad's favorite place in the world is Camp Aranzazu (www.camparanzazu.org). Camp Aranzazu is dedicated to enriching the lives of children and adults with chronic illnesses or special needs by providing unique camping or retreat experiences and environmental education to them. Mom and Dad helped start the camp and still give money and time to it. They do love God's special children! At the camp, ordinary activities like archery, ropes course, and the all-important Saturday Night Fever dance are provided to kids who are extraordinary. Campers who are blind can hit a bull's-eye at the archery range. Those who cannot walk can climb the tower and then soar on the zip line. I have watched kids who use wheelchairs play one mean game of hockey! Others who are deaf can line-dance in perfect unison to music they cannot hear. The Camp Aranzazu staff members adapt the activities to meet the needs of a camper. It is truly a magical place that focuses on what a camper can do instead of what limitations he or she may have. The name *Aranzazu* comes from a Bosque term that means "a spiritual place requiring a difficult path to reach." Those who attend or visit Camp Aranzazu are often on difficult paths; the campers with disabilities or illnesses obviously are on difficult paths. But what I found as I nurtured those who attended the camp is the camp counselors, doctors, staff members, and volunteers who attend with or serve the campers are often on difficult paths as well. I mean, really, who of us has *not* been on a difficult path? Fail a test? Hate to share a room with your brother? Can't handle your work or school load? Overwhelmed with rambunctious children or with life in general? Each of those is a difficult path. Walk, trot, or drive through those gates, and you too can find a spiritual place. I can testify to that experience as I have felt it myself. Part of my, Mom's, and Dad's hearts will always be at that special place.

The Bottom Line for Those Seeking Extraordinary Love

I hope you will find your own passion and give yourself to it financially and physically. Put someone else first. Try some of the services Mom and Dad love with children or adults with special needs, or consider rocking sick babies at a hospital. How about playing checkers with the elderly or delivering food to them? Or what about serving in a place near and dear to my own heart—an animal shelter?

Maybe a museum or soup kitchen for the homeless is the perfect place for you to volunteer.

My point is that there is no one place that is perfect for everyone, but there is one place that is perfect for you. Find it and give your heart and time and money to it; that is true extraordinary love!

CHAPTER 2

Love of Self

I believe that if you are going to take care of someone else, you have to take care of yourself first. Like the airlines say, put on your oxygen mask first before you assist others. I do understand the somewhat-common martyr attitude that some people have. They are caring, giving people who are often quite selfless. Yet by continually caring for others and not for themselves, they often end up losing their own health. Then they cannot help the people they truly love. Sometimes they end up resenting the very people they are trying help. So take my word for it—You cannot always put yourself first, but sometimes, you just need to. You have to fill your own cup. When yours is overflowing, it will be easy for you to fill everyone else's.

I learned from Mom and Dad that taking care of yourself—physically, mentally, emotionally, and spiritually—is the important start to experiencing extraordinary love. After all, who feels like loving anything when they don't feel good about themselves?

Physical Health

When I lived in the shelter, I did not have the opportunity to run much. I was one of the free dogs and was not kenneled, but I still lived inside boundaries and did not have enough space to show off my natural speed and agility. My love of running developed and expanded when Mom and Dad adopted me, and they took me on their daily training runs. I am *fast*! Surprisingly, I am also slow because even though I can run fast, I love to stop and smell the clover. Spring is my slowest season, but I digress. Because of my love for running, I eventually became the trainer. Mom and Dad were very much into fitness and health long before they met each other and before they met me. Then they developed a lifelong habit with each other (and with me, their trainer). Once I came along, morning walks and runs were never skipped. They learned to integrate our morning exercise into whatever schedule they had. They exercise and feed their bodies good, nutritious food. They also share a love for wine or an excellent margarita, and we all see that as a good thing!

Mental Health

It is important to also take care of your mental health. Have you ever heard the old adage that says that if you are not growing, you are dying? Keep your brain in shape! Mom and Dad love crossword puzzles. Mom is a voracious reader. They are continuous learners. They like to learn about different countries, different fitness and health strategies, different work-related subjects, and many other topics. They want to learn sign language and Spanish. Mom wants to take piano lessons; Dad wants to learn to play the fiddle. Those are just some of their goals. Remember, it is as important to exercise your brain as it is to exercise your body.

Emotional/Spiritual Health

I include these two together because they are so closely linked and Mom believes you cannot gain one without the other. To be happy, your emotions and spirit need to be healthy. Mom and Dad have been longtime churchgoers, which helps to nurture their spiritual health. It gives them something to believe in, which offers hope—something that helps them feel happy. They also experience emotional nurturing and spiritual healing in nature. The universe is an amazing spiritual teacher, and you will read much more about those experiences in the nature chapter.

The Bottom Line for Those Seeking Extraordinary Love

Find a way to fill your cup. Start an exercise program. If no one wants to go to your choice of movie, go by yourself! Get a massage. Take a class. Learn a new language. Go to church. Walk on the beach. Volunteer somewhere. Stay up all night on a blanket and admire the moon and stars with someone you love. Lock the door and take a long hot bubble bath (baths are not my personal favorite, but you have to find what is nurturing for you). Make time to fill your own cup, and you will find the time and energy you need to fill the cups of those around you.

CHAPTER 3

Love of Family

Even In-Laws, Ex-Laws (Outlaws?), and Friends

You would not believe how many people are in my family. I have more brothers and sisters and cousins and aunts and uncles and grandparents and nieces and nephews and other kids in my family than any one person can count without a calculator. Mom says you need a spreadsheet to keep up with who is who in our pack ("pack" is dog-speak for *family*). I refuse to learn math or anything even remotely related to a spreadsheet, so I am just going to describe the pack to you.

Family

The short story is this: In our family, it does not matter how you got here. If you are here, you are family.

And now for the long story—the one you might need a spreadsheet for. Dad's parents were married for over sixty years before they died. They raised three children, although some would argue that they raised thousands since both of them were teachers. Regardless of the number, their home pack stayed the same until others married into it. Dad was the baby and grew up in his older sisters' pack; he was such a cute baby! They are a beautiful example of extraordinary love.

Mom came from a different background. Her parents divorced when she was fourteen, and they brought new family members into the pack. Some people might call this a broken home, but she learned that it is actually an opportunity for expanded love and, dare I say it, extraordinary love! I think that you will agree with this soon enough as you read more about their stories and how they beautifully intertwine.

While Mom and Dad came from different backgrounds, they each exemplify perfect examples of extraordinary love.

Each of them has siblings who share their blood. Dad has two sisters with whom he grew up in Dallas, and I am pretty sure that living with girls taught him how to be an awesome husband and dad. Even when he didn't get girls, he got Mom. On the other side of Texas, near Corpus Christi, Mom grew up with a lot of brothers, and I am pretty sure that living with boys taught Mom how to be an awesome wife and mom. It also taught her to be tough, but that's another story.

Mom also has siblings who were adopted into the family. So here is where a spreadsheet might come in handy, but I'm not going to provide one, so pay attention! Mom has a mom and dad, but she also has her other mom. She has three brothers who share her blood, and she also has two adopted brothers who share the blood of her other mom. In addition, she has another brother and a sister who were adopted into the family. So if you are keeping up, you know that Mom has six brothers and one sister. Some people label those additional relationships as steps, but *my* mom says there is no such thing as a step. She thinks too many people think negatively on that word. She says that you can use the word if you need to clarify someone on a spreadsheet but not to describe a relationship. In our family, once you are in the family, you are in the family. It does not matter how you got here.

With the next generation, Mom and Dad were married first to other people and then divorced, and both of them were single for a long time before they met. They are soulmates and laugh-mates and like to say that God smiles on second chances, and as a rescued shelter dog, I know firsthand that that is true. I think we all rescued each other, and we will talk more about this in future chapters.

Mom and Dad share three children. At the time of this writing, they are blessed with nine grandchildren and are hoping for one or two more! Of the current grandkid pack, four share their blood, three are adopted, and two were lucky enough to marry into my family (yes, I am biased). Every single one of those children is uniquely special and beautiful, and Mom and Dad love them all dearly. I personally love it when they are all at my house at the same time! It is a bit chaotic, and they wear me out, but goodness, talk about feeling extraordinary love; it just flows through our house. I promise to share more about the love of children, especially these children, in a later chapter.

In-Laws, Ex-Laws, and Outlaws

Have you ever heard anyone talk negatively about their in-laws? I hear it a lot when I walk through town. I am sure some people are justified in their complaints, but I suggest it is because of actions and not because of the label *in-law*. Mom and Dad chose to love each other and all the family members (in-laws) that come with their relationship. They are blessed to be surrounded by amazing family members, including the in-laws. Even though they do not always agree with or share the opinions of other family members, they always respect them.

Even more common and very sad is when people talk badly about ex-laws—people who were once your chosen family but now are not legally family because of divorce. Mom learned a lot from her parents when they divorced; she learned about how one should treat people who were once their family but now are not. It once again boils back down to it not mattering how you got into a family. Mom and Dad have learned to find the good in all people, and that results in them having a much more enjoyable, much less stressful life. It is truly a life full of extraordinary love.

I can think of two strong examples of extraordinary love that come from in-laws and ex-laws. My paw-paw and grandma (Mom's parents) divorced long before I was born. Yet forty years later, when my grandma died, my paw-paw and my other grandma were at her funeral. My mom's former in-laws were at my grandma's funeral too. The same thing happened in October 2017—when in-laws and ex-laws (and quite a few outlaws) came together in a similar way to celebrate the life of someone very close to me, and I will talk more about it later. To me, those events show how much respect and how much love are in our family.

Friends (Some of Whom Are Outlaws)

Mom and Dad have amazing friends. Dad kept up with his friends from his junior high, high school, college, and early work days. Those guys are truly his brothers. They fished together and told really big fish stories. Mom and I rolled our eyes but not in front of the guys, so please do not tell them. Mom also has many dear friends who look out for her and do not hesitate to give assistance when she needs help. Dad understands Mom's need for her friends, and she encourages his friendships as well. I don't think Dad has ever rolled his eyes though; he just gets it. Friends are family—even if some of them earned outlaw reputations because of their crazy antics.

It is rare to find a traditional family these days. Divorce, death, abuse, abandonment, and other unfortunate situations can lead to broken homes and split families. Mom and Dad, though, decided early on that the circumstances that caused their split homes did not need to have a negative effect on them or their children. They felt pain, for sure, but they acknowledged it, nurtured their healing, and moved on. Because they had so much love inside of them, they saw the brokenness around them as an opportunity to expand their love to even more people. Like the Japanese tradition of Kintsugi, which means "golden joinery," Mom and Dad see beauty in what is broken. They repair brokenness with melted gold in the form of love so it becomes even more beautiful than before it was damaged. I have learned so much from them, and just for the record, I don't need a spreadsheet to keep up with the love I feel for all my family and friends—in-laws, ex-laws, and outlaws included.

The Bottom Line for Those Seeking Extraordinary Love

Open your heart and thoughts to the idea that a broken home (or a broken world) can offer opportunities to expand your love rather than diminish it. Refuse to feel bitter. Forgive those who do not ask for forgiveness—whether they deserve it or not. Reach out to someone who could use a friend. Once you open your mind and broaden your definition of who is family, you will also share the extraordinary love that I have experienced.

CHAPTER 4

Love of a Child

This chapter is not about loving a specific child or even about feeling the love of children. It is about the unfiltered, extraordinary love *within* a child. My goodness, the laughter! We can all learn from such raw, innocent, unrestrained joy.

Have you ever watched kids play? I am not talking about watching them to make sure they don't climb something or eat something that hurts them. I am talking about *really* watching them. Have you observed how they get along or how they sometimes don't get along, but that's okay because in five minutes, they get along again? They do not worry about how people perceive them; they just play. They are themselves—unfiltered and unencumbered by other people's perceptions or expectations. Yet when they get older, children somehow lose that innocence and joy. Adult hoomans filter their actions and attempt to sort thoughts to conform to society's perceived norms. I know that it is sometimes necessary for grown-ups to act, well, grown-up. But I also know that grown-ups will benefit from learning how to act like children again.

Mom has a picture of a little two-year-old baby on her desk. Grace is Mom and Dad's first grandchild. In the photo, she is in a field of bluebonnets. She is not looking at the camera, but she is also not looking at the bluebonnets. Who knows what she was thinking about at the time? Maybe the bluebonnets were pretty, or maybe a butterfly caught her eye? But something or someone made that baby look up and smile. And the joy and awe in her eyes are immeasurable. It is my favorite picture (next to the one of me and Dad driving, but that is another story). You look into those deep-blue eyes, and you can see and feel pure, unadulterated joy.

Here is a sidenote: Did you catch what I just said? Let this sink in—I used the word *unadulterated*. Have you ever thought about the meaning of that word? *Un-adult-erated*. Maybe we should all think about becoming unadulterated every now and then.

William is the first grandchild I knew as a baby. He and I met when he was about eighteen months old and I was ten months old. This special meeting took place during the week I was first adopted. So you might say we are really close to the same age and we get each other. Back then, we stood nose to nose! I remember a time when we were at the movie theater, taking William to his first movie. He was probably three, and I was probably two-and-a-half. Well, okay, I was not *really* there. But William later told me about a conversation he had with GT. By the way, GT is short for Grandpa Tracy. Dad used GT because he thought it was "sportier, ya know, than Grandpa." I am starting to figure out their naming theme, but I digress. Now back to the story.

William was at his first real movie. He sat in GT's lap the entire time, and he told me he was enthralled by the movie. Remember that he was only three years old, so he probably did not use the word *enthralled*; that is my description of how he was when he told me the story. GT was giving him snacks, and Nonnie (my mom) was there too. All of a sudden, in the middle of the movie, William burst out loud for everyone around to hear, "I just love you guys!" Really? Who does that? How many adults would be better people if someone would just burst out in the middle of a movie and tell them they are loved? Mom and Dad told that story for a long time. And I am still quite fond of hearing it. I love the pure, unadulterated joy of children.

Cousins Madeline and Kora are very special young ladies. They exemplify unfiltered, unadulterated joy in *everything*. They love mismatched socks and performing in public. They don't care how their vivaciousness makes them look to other people. Both of them can find the positive in any situation and in any person. They immediately embrace and love anyone they come across—well, except for maybe their respective brothers. I am truly delighted to be around those girls.

Grace and Khloe are the oldest of Mom and Dad's grandchildren. They are more refined and show their love differently than the rest of the kids. They are quiet and reserved. Extremely smart, you can tell when their brains are working; they take time to process things before they speak. They are a lot smarter than I am and much more controlled. I tend to run first and think later, and those two girls are the exact opposite of me. Yet they also exude unadulterated excitement when they are anticipating events that are important to them. I am glad they have not lost the joy of childhood.

Mom and Dad's grandchildren are living proof that God made his children to be different and made them all to be perfect. I am not biased at all when I state that they are unequivocally perfect!

The Bottom Line for Those Seeking Extraordinary Love

Seek out children! Watch them play and interact. Join their imaginary games. Experience their joy. Run in the grass with bare feet. Find something that makes you belly-laugh. Backtrack a bit to your own childhood. Find that extraordinary love that is within all children before the world takes it out of them. Encourage the children and adults around you to resist the ordinary world and to become extraordinary. Connect with *your* inner child. All hoomans and dogs have one. Find yours!

CHAPTER 5

Love of Nature

This chapter could have been combined with the one that talks about the love of God or included in the emotional/spiritual health section, but nature is just too special. Mother Nature needs her own chapter. Just for the record, I am an expert on nature; my sniffer can smell out natural beauty in a heartbeat!

Every Day in Nature

My favorite place to sniff is along the beach. Mom and I take a walk almost every day along a bay. We watch the sea birds and shore birds and often see jumping dolphins or schooling fish. We usually start our walk when it is still dark so we can also watch the sun rise in the sky over the water in Rockport, Texas. We do get some spectacular sunrises! God's canvas in the sky is filled with color and imagery. I never tire of it. I am definitely a beach babe.

My second favorite place to sniff is in my own backyard! We live in a beautiful area that boasts of coastal palms and majestic oak trees and a pond—all of which attract a ton of deer and birds. I used to chase the deer, but I figured out pretty quickly that they are bigger than me (and sometimes they are meaner too!), so now we just cautiously coexist. Mom and Dad's favorite date activity is just to sit on the back porch and watch the deer play. Every year, we have baby fawns and ducklings too; they are just adorable. We get to watch the sunset from our back porch—a time when the sky once again becomes vivid with colors.

Frogs, lizards, and other insects are even more abundant in our yard than the deer and birds. As a result, I have become a master lizard hunter. I love to stick my nose in bushes and flush them out. Then I chase them just for fun. I don't hurt them; we just play together. Sometimes they run up a tree, and I try to climb it, but I have not mastered that skill yet. Mom and Dad's grandsons, though, are almost as good as I am at hunting lizards and frogs, and they can even catch them thanks to their hands and opposable thumbs. William, Johnathon, and Tyler can climb the trees too. Korbin and Kinsler, the youngest of the pack, are coming right along as lizard-hunter trainees. The older boys and I are teaching the younger ones how to be careful with the bugs. We all love being outside together.

The Sky

Look up! There is so much beauty in the sky. No matter what time of day or night, you can find something spectacular in the sky. On a clear day, it looks like the sky goes on for miles. It is a perfect color of blue, just like my dad's eyes. If there are clouds, you can often find images within the clouds. I have seen clouds in the shape of squirrels and lizards. Mom often sees God, and that mermaid mom of mine can identify an ocean critter in any shaped cloud.

On a stormy day, you can experience an example of just how powerful nature is. You probably figured out by now that I am not a typical dog, so you may rightly assume that I am not a scaredy-cat when it rains. Instead, I enjoy a good rainstorm. I curl up on my bed, which is next to a window, and sleep right through thunder and lightning. I know that after almost every rainstorm, we go for a walk! The grass is so green after a good rain. It is like Mother Nature washed everything off! And my goodness, the smells! Our local park after a good rainstorm must be what heaven smells like. Everything is clean and fresh, and the frogs and lizards get drunk on it. I feel like a young pup whenever I go exploring after a rain. If I can't find the lizards and frogs, I will frolic in a mud puddle or two. Sometimes Mom and Dad join me, depending on how new their shoes are.

Yet think about this—all the experiences shared so far occurred during the day! How fantastic is it that we have a spectacular sky at night as well? How many times do you walk outside after dark and look up? Do it tonight! Count the stars. Stare at the moon. Watch the sun set or rise. I must admonish you to not stare at the sun, please. Mom's code prohibits it, and I bet that you too have been warned by your mom.

One of Mom and Dad's first dates happened in the middle of the night; they watched a meteor shower. They met at three in the morning in a large park by the bay. They counted hundreds of shooting stars. If you are a believer in luck, like I am, you know that their luck increased with every star. Thankfully, they met before I was born because I do not appreciate 3:00 a.m. wake-up calls. But I bet that if they wanted to do it again and take me with them, I would learn to appreciate the glory of the night sky. It would be my reward.

Mountains

Wow. As I said earlier, I am definitely a beach babe and not a snow bunny. But when you take one look at the majestic mountains, you just have to sit back and admire God's handiwork. There is so much life in them! The evergreen trees growing on the side of the mountain are so tall your neck hurts when you try to see their tops. Wildlife is abundant; deer and elk wander along the hillside, and you have to wonder—how the heck do those huge creatures not fall off the mountain? Mountain springs and waterfalls are my personal favorites; they are cold and refreshing all year. While wonderful all the time, especially splendid are the streams and falls when they freeze in the winter. Frozen waterfalls are mesmerizing. They are not only a treat to the visible eye, but if you sit quietly, you can also hear the water flowing in the streams underneath the ice. The ice itself is amazingly gorgeous as it becomes a prism of light. The waterfalls are not just ice-colored, as you might justifiably think if you have never seen frozen waterfalls or streams. Instead, they pick up hues of blue, and when the sun shines on them, they even sparkle with glitter. Even this beach babe can appreciate such beauty.

The Underwater World

Beach babes. I've mentioned it before, but it deserves repeating—my mom and I are authentic beach babes. When you get to know my mom and examine her life a little deeper, you see that her love of the water goes even beyond the beach. As I mentioned before, she is a mermaid. She loves to scuba dive and has been diving for almost thirty years. She has said many times that she meets with God underwater as often as in church. And that is saying something because she loves going to church!

Any of our earth's oceans is my mom's happy place. She loves to fish and loves to kayak. And she loves to fish from her kayak. (Get the connection?) Mom's favorite time of day while she is in her favorite place is sunrise. She perceives those sunrises as God smiling on us every morning. Similarly, Mom believes that the magnificent sunsets are portraits of God's glory.

Then *under* the water, she becomes a mermaid. She loves to float along quietly and observe the prolific life found under the sea—from the largest shark to the tiniest, little shrimp. She adores swimming along with no sounds other than the low gurgle of her bubbles escaping her regulator and the sounds of the parrotfish chomping on the coral. She is fascinated by how intricately the ocean critters fit together and serve each other.

Mom's favorite diving spot is in the Caribbean Sea. The visibility is easily one hundred feet, and the colors are vivid. The ocean ranges from bright turquoise to deep blue, and you can find every color under the sun in the fish and coral formations. The coral formations look like underwater mountains reaching for the sky, and a plethora of sea creatures dart in and out of the anemones. It truly is majestic.

The Unexpected Power of Nature

You might remember that I began penning this book in 2017, during the aftermath of Hurricane Harvey. The hurricane hit on a Friday, August 25, 2017, and the eye went directly over Rockport, Texas—my hometown. During our walks, Mom always talks about the power of nature. Sometimes the bay is really churned up, and sometimes it is calm. Sometimes the sea wears diamonds—when the sun glistens on the gentle waves. Other times, the sea is just angry, and the waves beat on each other. Sometimes it is really windy, and sometimes it is not. But the angriest sea rolled in with Harvey, who struck us as a strong category 4 storm with 130-miles-per-hour winds. We stayed home during the hurricane because my dad was sick and we could not evacuate. We stayed up all night and listened while the wind howled; it sounded like a lady screaming. It was really creepy, but unlike other dogs, I am not a storm scaredy-cat. I just sat with Mom and Dad and listened. And I took lots of much-needed naps. It didn't take long for the power to go out, and it was dark outside and inside. We lit candles and just listened. We heard trees breaking and debris flying.

We were very lucky that our home and office only suffered minimal damage, but the rest of Rockport was not so fortunate. Many people lost their homes and businesses, and numerous others had to leave town. The last I heard, it will take five years for Rockport to get back to the number of residents and businesses it had on August 24, 2017.

When the storm was over the next day, we went for a little drive. I normally love to go on a car ride, but this time, I could sense Mom's nervousness. First, we had to clear trees from our driveway just to get the truck out of the garage. Then we didn't even have to leave the block before I saw it. The community damage was massive. Harvey definitely was powerful and painted a picture of devastation that I had never seen before. There were downed power lines everywhere. We saw homes without roofs and some homes without walls. We saw concrete slabs, and we couldn't remember the buildings that were there the day before. Businesses and homes and, more importantly, livelihoods were destroyed. Mom cried out loud as she drove, although I know she was trying to hide her tears from me. I whimpered a bit, supporting her and knowing deep down the meaning of it all; I knew this was not good.

We had to take a deep, long breath.

After we exhaled and really started to pay attention, we noticed nature start her healing immediately. Some of our flowers were blown out of our flower bed, and within a few weeks, they sprang up in the yard close by! Our neighbors' flowers are now blooming in *our* yard—bouquets of color that we did not plant ourselves. The trees that were blown down made room for the remaining trees and grass to get more sun and nutrients, and they are now green, fresh, and thriving. Mom's friend Tommy lost his home and part of his business, but when we walked past his house on the first spring after Harvey, a gorgeous bed of Easter lilies were growing in his front yard. Those lilies framed an unlivable home without a roof or walls. Mom told me that it was a photograph that depicts the juxtaposition of heartache and hope. And I believe her. Tommy has since rebuilt his home in the same place, and I kept an eye on the contractor to ensure that they protected the lilies.

Mom has an innate appreciation and downright awe for nature, and I can sense it too. There is nothing more magnificent than how wonderful and powerful nature is.

The Unexpected Power of Nature—Again!

If you live in far South Texas, like we do, you know it has a very warm climate. Many of us don't even own a winter coat. Mom loves how she wears shorts on Thanksgiving and Christmas more often than she wears a sweater. Those of us who choose to live here love this warm weather! The warm climate allows me, a somewhat-active hound dog, to lie around on the back porch and slobber lazily and blame it on the climate, not on my personality. I am sure I would be an Olympic athlete-dog in a cooler climate, but here, I am Mom and Dad's temperature gauge. If I don't move, it is too hot. 'Nuff said.

But once again, I digress. We will get back to the power of nature and the juxtaposition of the summer and fall of 2017, but we need to touch on a little history first. It snowed in South Texas in 2004—the first time in almost one hundred years. Mom said they thought it was a once-in-a-lifetime event. It happened on Christmas Eve and was called a South Texas miracle. The kids forgot about Santa and went out to play in the snow. My church pastor was taking snowballs to the face while he was still in the church after the Christmas Eve service! Dad played out his lifelong fantasy of catching the football for the winning touchdown while diving into the snow. If you live in a snowbound universe, you don't understand the significance of what I am saying. But if you live in the south, you get me.

So now we get back to 2017. Hurricane Harvey was the first hurricane to hit the Rockport area in over forty years. Harvey alone was a notable, historic weather event. But what do you know, just four short months after Hurricane Harvey hit, we had—wait for it—*snow*! We had about seven inches of fresh snow. The snow is even more evidence of the power of nature. Think about it—We had a hurricane and a snowfall in the same year within four months of each other. Who does that? Mother Nature was just showing off her crazy side! And in spite of my disliking the snow, I did appreciate the excitement that was shown by Mom and the rest of our neighborhood.

Now remember, I am a beach babe, not a snow bunny. I wanted nothing to do with the snow. Mom was laughing and taking pictures and making snowballs, and I just wanted it to melt so I could have my green grass back and do my normal business. Call me a scrooge; I am fine with that. But all around our town, kids, adults, and more adventurous dogs were outside, playing in the snow, just like Mom was. Even though I don't like the cold or snow, I have to admit that pure joy had returned to South Texas! The process of recovering from a hurricane is long and hard; it takes years for some people to return to normal. It takes a toll on people financially, physically, and emotionally. And four months after Harvey, people were tired. I ran across many who were also quite cranky. And then nature sent us this unexpected gift, a snow-wrapped box, and inside it was a cleansing, healing blanket. People were in a good mood again. They still had to go back to their post-Harvey lives and continue the recovery effort, but this snow miracle was just what our community needed to be forced to take a break and appreciate life and nature.

The Bottom Line for Those Seeking Extraordinary Love

Dare I say it? Does it even need to be said? It is so simple—Learn to love and appreciate nature! Shut down the electronics. Turn off the TV. Simply go outside! Watch the sun rise or set. Feel the ocean as it ebbs and flows. Listen to the sea (she has much wisdom), and watch the sea glitter (remember, she wears diamonds)! Walk through the grass without shoes. Admire the night sky. Make a date to watch a meteor shower in the middle of the night. Work in the garden without gloves. Get dirty! Appreciate a thunderstorm. Take time to shut down and use your senses to appreciate the nature that envelops you. Develop an extraordinary love for nature. It is around us all the time, and it can change your life. I know that it changed mine.

CHAPTER 6

Love of Strangers—and Strangeness

This chapter is all about loving the strangers and strangeness that are in our world. I encourage you to pay attention to the love and the craziness that are out there. If we just pay attention, we will see so much more of the good in people than the negative that we sometimes tend to focus on.

Love of Strangers—Random Acts of Kindness

Have you ever had a stranger pay for your coffee without telling you? Mom remembers a time many years ago when a man bought our pizza. It made her day! That moment in time was more than twenty-five years ago (okay, maybe it was not *my* pizza), but it changed Mom's life, and she will never forget it. She recognized then how good it feels to be the recipient of a random act of kindness, and she strives to find ways to pay it forward. She often will pay for someone's coffee or dessert, and sometimes she will even splurge on a whole dinner for a family she admires. She is a sucker for families with rambunctious kiddos.

Random acts of kindness don't always have to cost money. A different act of kindness came after Hurricane Harvey. After the storm, cell service in our town was almost nonexistent—except for on the top of an overpass on our little bypass highway. Mom was out there, trying to text updates to the family, as were a couple of dozen other people. One man came up to her and struck up a conversation. They shared their hurricane stories, and the man asked if he could pray for Mom and Dad. He prayed that even if Mom could not see the entire road ahead of her, she would always know exactly what her next step should be. Mom has been reminded of that prayer when she is scared or not sure of what is in our future. She didn't get his name but is convinced that he was her hurricane angel.

There are so many stories of kindness that came from the hurricane. Those stories could make up a whole other book! People who lost everything were helping their neighbors clean up debris and rebuild homes. Other people came from all over the United States to help us recover. In the midst of such heartbreak and turmoil, there was so much joy and hope. Some people say that life is bad and people are always out to get you and tear you down. Mom says the reverse is true and that this is the way life ought to be and truly is—we help each other, and we build each other back up. And we saw this firsthand! People helped us clean up the yard and house in order to get them safe and ready. Strangers helped us get funds for the hotel and repairs. Mom and Dad are such givers; it was hard for them to be on the receiving end of help this time. But that help fed their souls and lifted their spirits, supporting them for the harder days yet to come.

Love of Strangeness

I just had to throw this short section into the book. I love strangeness! One day, Mom and I were driving through town and saw a grown woman, probably in her fifties, riding a bicycle through town in a skimpy little bikini. You could kind of see her, well, everything. Mom and I looked away, then looked back at her again, then looked away and grinned at each other. We said in unison, "You go, girl!"

One of our neighbors walks through our town with a huge backpack. On top of the backpack rides a tiny, little dog. I don't know how many miles he walks in a day, but every time we see him, that little dog is as happy as can be. I would like to ride on top of a backpack someday. I weigh eighty-two pounds, though, so I am not sure if that can happen, but I would like to try nonetheless!

There have been other people we have seen who sometimes feel a bit strange—primarily because they are different from us. But by learning to embrace and enjoy that strangeness, we have found a great appreciation for all the differences that bring color and diversity to our world. We know that everyone has a story that they are telling through their dress, actions, and antics. We also know that everyone deserves to tell their story in whatever fashion best suits them!

The Bottom Line for Those Seeking Extraordinary Love

Try accepting situations and people for what and who they are. Embrace strangers and strangeness! Start paying attention to opportunities. Let someone else have that parking place. Pay for someone's meal. Ride through town in a bikini! (But don't break the law, please.) Do something nice for a stranger. Dance on the sidewalk. Open the door for the person behind you. Carry someone's groceries. Mom loves to do random acts of kindness whenever she can. You probably have heard of the concept of paying it forward. What you may not know is that what you pay forward comes back to you tenfold. It will grow your heart.

CHAPTER 7

Love of Animals
(Finally! My Own Chapter!)

Yes, all dogs *do* go to heaven. And so do horses, cats, guinea pigs, fish, and other beloved critters—but not mosquitoes. Definitely not mosquitoes!

I know without a doubt that all dogs, cats, and other beloved pets go to heaven. The love I feel for my mom and dad is so strong, it must come from God; this must mean that I will get to go to heaven. I can't imagine a heaven without pets in it. Can you? I never get mad at my parents—even when they get mad at me (through no fault of my own, of course). I am a dog, so I obviously think that dogs are the best. But I do know that there are other pets that love their humans. Cats have a hard time showing it, but you can't help but feel the love when they curl up and purr next to you, or so I've heard. I have never curled up next to a cat. Even though I believe they go to heaven, I am equally convinced that they have cooties.

My mom and dad are pretty happy people, but every now and then, they have a bad day. When that happens, I go into healing mode. I can fix whatever is bothering them! I will take them for a walk, or we will play with my ball to clear our heads. Or I will shake my drool so it covers my big nose—they really like that one. They laugh every single time. Mom says it is a face only a mother could love, but I know Dad gets a kick out of me too.

Did you know that there is even a thing called puppy therapy? I made up the term, but it is a very powerful healing event. If you have not already experienced the joy of puppy therapy, I highly recommend that you try it. On your worst day, throw yourself into the midst of half a dozen puppies and attempt not to laugh. You won't be able to do it; the rules of puppy therapy will force you to giggle no matter how hard you try not to! Laughter produces feel-good hormones that will help you deal with your problems. I personally have very little patience for puppies, but I do understand why people think they are cute. So I get it—puppy therapy is very good for humans.

I have not heard of fish therapy or cat therapy, but I do know that there is such a thing as horse therapy. Horses provide therapeutic riding to many people with disabilities or special needs. How cool is that? Therapy aside, I think the main thing that you must understand is that you probably have an affinity to some kind of animal. Once you figure out which one it is, you will likely find therapeutic benefits from interacting with that kind of animal.

The Bottom Line for Those Seeking Extraordinary Love

This one is simple and short: Get a pet! If you can't have a pet at your home, go walk someone else's dog or volunteer at an animal shelter. The unconditional love of a pet will spill over and into you!

CHAPTER 8

Love of Emotion

Learning to Be Open and Vulnerable

All emotions are good. Yep, you heard me. All of them have a part to play in this life, and I have felt many of them—joy, fear, surprise, trust, anger, happy, sad, confused, helpless, anxious, feisty (my personal favorite), fascinated, frightened, thankful, baffled, thrilled, timid, heartbroken, sheepish, compassionate, and confused. Shall I go on?

If you answered "Yes" to that question, then I know without a doubt that I should go on! I feel the need to share with you the fact that I thought about omitting this chapter from the book. It was part of my original outline and something I admire in my mom (all those feelings!). But talking about emotions that many people label as negative just seemed daunting. But then someone (you know who you are) talked me into keeping it. And I know it is right to do so.

Many hoomans tend to think of emotions as good or bad—positive or negative. Happy is good; sad is bad. A loving heart is positive; a broken heart is negative. Any emotion that feels uncomfortable or stressful *must* be bad, right? Those who believe that some emotions are bad or negative seek to experience and feel only what they label as good. They don't want to feel sad. They don't want to feel angry or heartbroken or frightened. So they build walls around their hearts and souls and attempt to let in only the good emotions, avoiding any feeling that is labeled as bad.

47

But I challenge you to think about emotions the way I do. They are all good! They are what make us, us. People have emotions. So let's look at them a little deeper.

Happy

We all want to feel this way! I suspect that we all *do* feel this way. It is good to feel happy. Some people even spend their lives searching for happiness. But it is not possible to feel happy all the time. We need the yin and the yang—the happy and the sad.

Sad

As I write this, Mom is crying her eyes out. Her eyes are as red as my hound-dog eyes often are, but Mom's are much more wet. I don't really understand her tears, but I do understand that she needs me. I know her tears are cleansing, but I don't quite understand what causes them or how they make her better. I think she is sad right now. I have seen her this way before, and even I know it will not last. Her emotions will change.

And sometimes those emotions change in a way I do not like. I know my mom and dad love me. That is good. But I also know they will occasionally get mad at me for something I did wrong (usually through no fault of my own). So does that make anger bad? No. Anger is just anger. The way we respond can make it bad—just think about that. In this case, Mom and Dad's anger tells me something is wrong, and it teaches me boundaries. How can that be a bad thing?

I think we have a lot to learn about emotions.

Laughter

This deserves a section all to itself. A form of the word *laugh* appears in this book more than twenty times. This is no accident; laughter is important to our family, and it is important to me that you understand how important it is in our world. We could use a little more laughter in this broken world!

One of Mom and Dad's first dates included watching a goofy movie. Dad wanted to make sure that Mom would laugh. Now, mind you, this is a movie that only guys can truly appreciate, but she passed the test. Mom grew up with six brothers, so she is well acclimated to guy humor. As an only child with no brothers, I don't always understand the male brain, but Mom does. The story Dad tells is that she did laugh and he was smitten, although rumor has it that she also completed a few perfectly timed eye rolls as well. Yet I have a feeling that Dad thought those eye rolls were funny too. The moral of this story is that laughter brought my mom and dad together, and laughter helped keep them together—even during the hard times that will be detailed in other chapters.

Our family's affinity for acting goofy goes along with our love for strangeness, something you read about in a previous chapter. Mom is goofy. Dad is goofy. They love being goofballs together—when it is appropriate, of course! When they adopted me, I quickly got the nickname Goofy Girl. The reality is, sometimes goofiness just fits in this world that is often quite messy. I'm talking about the "dance or sing like no one is watching" kind of goofy. I do not know how to laugh or sing, although I have a lovely hound-dog howl that changes pitch depending on how excited I am. I do not know how to dance, but I sure can prance through the tall grass, and I have an awesome twirl when I am excited. Prancing and twirling are almost the same thing as dancing, right? I learned a lot from my parents. I embrace laughter and love being goofy. I hope you do too.

The Bottom Line for Those Seeking Extraordinary Love

Embrace your emotions! Laugh every day. If you feel sad, cry. If you feel embarrassed, laugh at yourself. If you feel happy, dance. If you feel goofy, dance in public. There is no perfect way to live in this world, but I do know that emotions come along for the ride; they are a given. If you try to squash what you are feeling, you are squashing your innermost self. So feel what you feel, and please laugh and dance anyway.

CHAPTER 9

Love of a Lover

If you chose this book based on just the title, I bet you thought this chapter would be first. Or maybe you anticipated that lovers would be the *only* topic in a book about love? But I hope you realize by now that it took seeking, finding, and appreciating the love of God, self, nature, family, children, and the other kinds of love represented in the rest of these chapters to get to lover's love. The practice of the first eight types can lead directly to the experience of a lover's love, as it did in my mom and dad's case. This chapter is about married love and specifically includes romantic/deep/pure love. It is about that kind of love that you get to *choose*. It is the kind of love that you act on, not a word you think you have to say or an emotion that you might get lucky enough to feel. Mom says that without all the kinds of love that are described in the rest of the chapters, she might have never recognized and appreciated the love she has for my dad.

Mom says *love* is a verb, not a noun. What? Many people I know believe that love is something you feel. While my mom appreciates the feeling, she opposes it as being the only expression of the word. She says *love* is really an action verb. Yes, she is adamant that you express love rather than feel love, although she does agree that feeling love is amazing! As a beloved hound dog, I must clarify that I need to *feel* love, and Mom is stretching me as I attempt to understand. She explained that every time I wag my tail and run to the door when they get home, I am expressing *love* as an action verb. Heck, I taught her to wag her tail when Dad came home from fishing, and she did with laughter and love while trying to outwag me! And can I say that Dad loved coming home because both of us were wagging our tails when he arrived? He appreciated that I taught Mom how to express love in that way.

How often have you heard the concept that states "Marriage is 50-50"? Or maybe you have heard the similar "Love is give-and-take"? My mom challenges those expectations. She taught me that relationships are not 50-50, nor are they give-and-take. By now, I suspect that you anticipate something better (or at least different) from my mom, and you are going to get it. She is confident that love is 100-100. If you say that love is 50-50, doesn't it imply that you are only giving half of yourself and expect only half of the other person? Wouldn't you rather be in a relationship with someone who is giving you their all—their 100 percent? Now please understand that I am realistic, and I recognize that 100 percent cannot happen all the time. No one can give 100 percent all the time, or they would be really tired and definitely would not be receiving. But all of us can strive for it, and when we fall short—and life and human nature dictate that we *will* fall short—we know our partner is giving enough to make up for the difference when we are tired and just have nothing else to give.

Mom feels the same about the give-and-take description about love and relationships. She thinks love should be give and *give*. She would admonish you to not go into your relationship while thinking about what you deserve or what you can get or *take* out of it. Just go into it while giving what you have, but go into it while planning and hoping to give. Many times, you will have 100 percent to give. Other times, you will have less. And sometimes, you get to be on the receiving end of the 100 percent that your lover wants to give to you.

So now that you know what Mom and Dad think about love, you can better understand how they treat each other. The rest of this chapter talks about how my mom and dad found the love of a lover. We can call it their love story!

Mom and Dad—Before They Met

I feel that in order for you to fully appreciate and truly enjoy the love story of my mom and dad, you have to know a little of their history. So I am going to give you the nuts and bolts of their history. Just for the record, I don't know what "nuts and bolts" means, but Dad says it a lot whenever I try to tell him a story, so I think it means "Get to the point."

My mom was married the first time when she was only sixteen years old and stayed married for almost thirteen years before her divorce. She was single for about eight years after the divorce before she met my dad. Dad was married before too, although he was not as young as Mom! Then he was divorced for well over ten years before he met Mom. They each had children from their first marriages—Mom had two daughters, and Dad had a son. They were co-parenting outside the box before it was a thing, and in my opinion, they did it well. Now they each have a great appreciation and respect for their former spouses, and they separately-yet-together raised three amazing adults, who are now raising nine spectacular kiddos. To set the stage and to confirm your math, Mom was thirty-six and Dad was almost forty-one when they met. They had three children between them; one had just started college, one was in high school, and the youngest was in middle school.

I mentioned earlier that Mom had been thinking about writing this book for many years. As we move forward, it might be interesting for you to know that she had already written the majority of this book in her mind when that magical day in January 2000 happened.

God Smiles on Second Chances

Not many people know how my mom and dad met because at the time, it was not a popular way, so they kept it to themselves. Grandma and Paw-Paw, you might want to skip this section. But for the rest of you, I will boldly and proudly proclaim it out loud: Mom and Dad met online!

Yes, you heard that right; they met online. But I must clarify this situation: This was before the days of the now-popular dating websites and before a few evil people had figured out how to manipulate the system. It happened before you heard about dangerous meetings. This was in the early days—when Yahoo had a personals section. At the time, Dad lived in Dallas, and Mom lived at a place in South Texas that is about thirty miles away from where we live now. Dad posted that he was looking for a running/training partner. He wanted someone who would diligently train with him. And (here's the kicker) he was looking for a female running partner. He said it was because women are more dependable than men. As a female, I know he was right. He also preferred someone who was an active Christian yet would drink a beer with him after the run.

On the day Dad posted this, Mom was looking around, bored with the rest of the ads. Then she saw Dad's search for the perfect running partner, and she typed this response: "Good luck with your search! She exists. She just lives 400 miles away."

I have to remind you that during that time, Dad could not look at a profile to see what Mom looked like or even how she presented herself in words. Profiles did not exist yet! But he was smitten then and there (and so was she). He responded to her. She responded back. They met in person within a month, and the rest is history. They like to say that they experienced love at first sight even though it took them almost four years to get married. I guess they just wanted to make sure of their sight! But their perfect love began with a shared interest in running, beer, and God (not exactly in that order).

Mom and Dad like to clarify that they *met* online; they did not *date* online. They agree that any way of meeting is good and often meant to be—online, through mutual friends, at church, or at a club. But they also believe that an interpersonal relationship has to start fairly quickly because being together in person is the only way to truly get to know a person. They are adamant that you cannot get to know a potential mate through a computer screen.

My parents dated long-distance for a couple of years. They met three weekends every month—one weekend in his town, one in her town, and one in a town they would pick that was between them (usually Austin). Then they would take a weekend off. This worked until they finally knew that their love was genuine and it was time to live in the same city. So Dad moved to Mom's town! While Dad was established in Dallas and enjoyed his job, he knew he would be happier on the coast than Mom would be in the concrete jungle. So he moved to Mom's town! And he sure was right. He fit in as a coastal boy right away. After Dad moved, they dated a bit longer while living in separate homes. A little more than three years after they met, Dad *finally* proposed. Everyone was so happy when they finally married almost four years after they met. Our preacher was truly overjoyed when he got to announce them as husband and wife!

God in a Marriage

Mom and Dad are soul mates. They know without a doubt that God brought them together. But almost as important to them (and maybe even important to God) is the fact that they are laugh-mates. Laughter is so important to them. Mom often claimed that she married Dad because she felt she was a better Christian with him in her life than she was without him. She also said more often, I'm afraid, that she married Dad because she laughed *at* him every day (although I'm pretty sure she meant *with*). Dad said he married Mom because she laughed at *and* with him! What a happy couple! They are just fun, and many people admire them. They also say that they prayed for each other before they ever even met. I think this is how they just knew that God orchestrated their union.

Mom and Dad met in January 2000 and married in September 2003. They had a lot of fun times during that time frame even though Mom said it took Dad forever to propose. But he did propose, and their marriage is one that many people admire. They played together, ran and fished together, and worked together to start and build up Dad's business. Mom and Dad continued to run together and enjoyed their shared love of fitness after they married. They adopted me in 2009—an event that became the highlight of their married life! Life was good.

Then things changed a bit. My dad was diagnosed with cancer in early 2011—only eleven years after they met, a very short seven years after they married, and only a couple of years after they adopted me. This diagnosis revealed itself in an emergent situation; my athlete dad was suddenly very sick.

But instead of thinking about himself, my dad was always looking out for my mom. When he was about to be sedated for his first surgery, he knew that Mom was scared. True to my dad's nature, if he was also scared, he didn't show it except for maybe a tiny tear on the outside of his left eye (but he does not know we saw it). Dad did not show his fear; instead, he told Mom that he knew without a doubt that he would be okay. He told her, "God didn't make me wait so long to find you just to take me from you now." Dad always believed that God had put them together and was not going to tear them apart!

A Family—Designed for God

Thank goodness for those second chances! My mom and dad will be the first to tell you that they think that God designed marriage till death parted the partners. And they did not achieve that goal with their first marriages. Instead, they truly believe that God also smiles on second chances. Mom and Dad's first marriages ended in divorce. It was not what they planned when they respectively married, but it is real life, and they were very saddened by it. When each of them got divorced, Mom had two daughters, and Dad had one son. They did not want to be divorced, yet they knew that it was the best recourse for their situations. They still hoped that God would show them his plan. And when Mom and Dad met and married, God smiled on their second chance. Their families are now intertwined. Mom's daughters are Dad's now. Dad's son is Mom's now. Mom and Dad recognize that their kids' other parents are primary role models and very important in our lives. We are grateful that Mom and Dad's adult children and grandchildren have many more people who love them thanks to God smiling on their second chance.

Give-Give

I have mentioned more than once in this book that Mom and Dad have a lover philosophy of give-give—100-100 (rather than 50-50). They not only believe that philosophy, but they also live it. During their years together, they were not always in the giving mode (who could be?), but they always tried. Most of the time, they love giving! They are not always comfortable with receiving, yet they knew that by receiving, they were giving a gift to the other.

The Bottom Line for Those Seeking Extraordinary Love

Reread this chapter. Pick up snippets of wisdom from the rest of my story. Let God help you find a lover; don't search for him or her. Searching causes too much stress! And when you do find that lover, live your relationship with an attitude of give-give. If you already have your lover and are seeking a better relationship, try that giving philosophy that my mom and dad have. Oh, and laugh.

CHAPTER 10

Love of Life

While the first nine chapters of my book include what Mom and Dad have learned about extraordinary love and how to find it, this chapter is mostly about my dad. He had cancer for six years—almost as long as I was alive at the time. In fact, I am pretty sure I diagnosed him long before the doctors did. I kept sniffing him, and I somehow knew that smell. Dad kept telling me to move on, but I just knew and tried to alert him. More than half of my life was spent with him as he went in and out of chemotherapy, alternative treatments, and multiple major surgeries. Even though Dad had cancer for so many years, almost no one else knew it because he lived life with such vigor and vitality. In spite of his illness, he crammed more life into fifty-eight years than most people do in ninety years. So this chapter is my tribute to him.

Dad died on a Sunday.

I remember it well. Dad died on September 24, 2017—just a week after Mom's birthday and only a few days after their wedding anniversary. When Dad started his hospice program many weeks earlier, he requested that only Mom and I be with him when he died. He had already said his good-byes to everyone else, and he wanted just us with him in those last days. So as we promised, only Mom and I were with him when he took his last breaths at home. Mom held him, and I was right by his side, resting my chin on the bed. I had never been allowed on our furniture and was usually not allowed to get my drool on any piece of it. But I wanted Dad to know that I was there for him, and Mom knew that my nearness to him was more important than the drool on the sheets. In his last moments, I think he knew we were there and we love him very much. And, my goodness, we miss him!

Dad's memorial service was a true celebration. There were tears, of course, but the spirit of extraordinary love was so evident, and there were even some laughs. We all knew how laughter was important to my dad—even at his funeral. Mom was so proud; I could tell. She loves him a lot—extraordinarily.

Dad—a Life Well Lived

The rest of this chapter includes parts of Dad's obituary, which reflects a lot of the best of him that was perceived by the people who loved him. And then I will share his final thoughts. Even when he was dying, he was thinking about the rest of us. That's my dad—always putting someone else first. He wanted us to know how he felt about us and, more importantly, how he felt about life. He claimed to be just an average guy, but I know he was an extraordinary man. And he is the poster child for extraordinary love. His message is one of hope, and I learned that no matter how sad we are or how frustrated with work or health or life in general we are, there is always, *always* hope.

My dad attended school in the Dallas and Frisco areas (those are in Texas, y'all) and retained many of the friends he made in those places for the rest of his life. He graduated from Baylor University. (Go Bears!) Dad always wanted to be an insurance agent, so he studied business and insurance at Baylor. After finishing college, he began his career in the insurance industry. He was not only an up-and-comer, but he also remained lifelong friends with many of the people that he met during those times. Dad was a genuine friend, and he attracted good people. When he made a friend, he kept that friend for life.

Dad worked in the insurance industry his entire career and eventually founded Risk Resources LLC. That is the only job that I knew my dad to have. He rarely left me home alone as his office was in our home. I helped him work as much as I could in between my naps. My dad built his agency the same way he lived his life—with an innate desire to always do the right thing and treat people with the utmost respect and care. He had an amazing work ethic.

Dad met my mom, his soul mate and laugh-mate, in the year 2000 (just for the record, I was born in the year 2009). They lived a life filled with love, laughter, family, and friends, and they shared a love for the water. As I mentioned earlier, after Dad met Mom, he moved from Dallas to the Texas Gulf Coast and was hooked (literally and figuratively). Dad was always a churchgoing boy, but he also met with God while fishing on Copano Bay, scuba diving in the Caribbean, playing with his grandchildren, and sitting on the back porch with Mom and me. I have never been allowed inside a church, but I sure do understand how God lives everywhere else that Dad met with him. My dad loved life and lived it to the fullest—wherever he was and whatever he was doing.

Remember, Dad named himself GT, short for Grandpa Tracy, because it is "sportier, ya know, than Grandpa." True to his name, GT was sportier than any other grandfather I have ever met! Many people were impressed and inspired by the twenty-four marathons he completed. He even ran the coveted Boston Marathon—twice! But people remember most the two marathons that he accomplished while he was on chemotherapy. Yes, my dad was a stud. I must be a stud too because I ran with Dad a lot. I suppose that you could call me his official trainer. Dad was fast and a successful athlete, yet he always said he was more proud of the discipline and determination it took to *train* for a marathon than he was of the actual race. In training and in life, he exemplified integrity. Yep, that's my dad.

Dad—His Final Thoughts

My dad wrote most of his funeral/memorial service. He chose the songs and the scripture verses. He also wrote part of the homily in the form of his final thoughts.

When Dad told our pastor, Milton, that he was going to write his final thoughts and Mom would read them at the service, it was the first time she'd heard of this; they had *not* discussed it! I was sitting right there at Dad's feet and know this is a fact. Milton and Susan, our other wonderful church friend, came over when Dad first started his hospice care. They gave him the Holy Eucharist and prayed with him and Mom, and more importantly, they just visited and were friends. They loved on me too and gave me treats, and they let me hang out and observe the situation, which you all know by now is so important to the telling of this book.

When Dad mentioned Mom reading his final thoughts, Mom's first reaction was "*What? No way I can do that!*" She looked at me like Dad was *crazy*! But then she remembered everything they had gone through to be where they were. She decided that this was the least she could do for him. I think this says a lot about their relationship and how he felt about her; he just assumed that she would be strong enough to do it. I personally knew that she could, but she needed to hear it from him too. I looked at them and saw again the 100-100 relationship that they had. This time, it was Mom's turn to give and Dad's turn to receive.

The rest of these words are Dad's thoughts. Mom read them at his memorial service, but they are presented here as if they are coming directly from him.

> Thanks to all of you for attending today. Funerals are not fun. But I want this farewell to feel more like a celebration of life. So I want to leave you with some thoughts—about my life and the way I chose to live it.
>
> Life is hard and not always fair. We all know that. At this time, it is easy to focus on loss and pain, BUT (as Dr. Phil would counsel, the only thoughts that count are after the BUT)... So, here is my life after the "but."

*I'd rather have 17 years with my cherished soul mate, Tammie, than 100 years with a less than fulfilling marriage.

*I'd rather take a risk and experience the thrill of the unknown (good or bad) than play it safe and live a lesser quality life.

*I'd rather find one nicked Titleist than 10 pristine Top Flite golf balls.

*Laughter is important. Tammie and I laughed every day. Sometimes with each other, and sometimes at each other. But we laughed— and were better and stronger for it.

*I have faith in the promise of eternal life given by our Creator and Jesus Christ. I expect that afterlife to be much different, yet more fulfilling than anything I could have ever imagined.

Mom had to interject something when she was reading Dad's final thoughts. She told the crowd that a few days before Dad died, he was talking to someone we could not see. Mom asked him who he was talking to, and he got this huge grin on his face and said, "To God." So then she asked him, "Are you getting to see heaven?" His grin got even bigger, and he said, "Oh, Tams, this is good. I am going to miss you. But this is so, so good." Mom said she will never forget the look of sheer joy on his face, and neither will I. My dad was my first introduction to heaven, and there is no doubt in my mind that it is where he is right now.

Let's go back to Dad's final thoughts. The rest of these words are from him.

*I would not trade my friends, family, or any of my experiences with them—for anything.

Finally, I would like to share one of my life's epiphany moments with you. It happened at a Cursillo, which is a type of spiritual retreat, on Mustang Island. Bishop Folts was a former

Baptist, turned Episcopalian, turned Bishop—
just like me (except for the Bishop part)! We had
similar upbringings, and I had a great affinity for
him—then gained great respect. All who know
him love him, and when he speaks, people listen.

He has a great speaking style of hesitating at
just the right moment. Well, at Cursillo, he was
giving a talk, and he hesitated. You could hear a
pin drop as everyone leaned in to hear his next
words. He said,

"Having hope vs. having despair is a choice."

I will say that again—having hope vs.
having despair is a choice. It is *not a feeling*. So
despair for a moment for me if you need to—I
know that is natural, especially today. But please
don't stay there—don't let despair paralyze you.

I chose hope during every one of the battles
I had with cancer—and there were many more
remissions and reoccurrences than I could count.
But with every one, I chose hope—hope of cure,
hope of more time with my family and friends,
hope of living—and I mean really living—not
just being alive. And I hope now, if my life is a
testimony to anything, it is an example of hope
and faith in God and in all that is good.

Cheers, my friends. I'll see you on the other
side.

I don't know how I can add any more to this tribute for my dad.
He lived his life with integrity and grace, and the world is a better
place because he was here. I love him—extraordinarily.

The Bottom Line for Those Seeking Extraordinary Love

My dad crammed a whole lot of living into his fifty-eight years on this earth. Do you wonder if you can live as fully as he did? I promise that you *can*! I can only hope that you will listen to him and take his advice to heart. Go back and read his thoughts again. Which part of his advice can you put into action now? What is one thing that you can do today? What mind-set can you change?

EPILOGUE

(This final chapter was written by my mom.)

I am grateful to GG for writing her story. I trust that you realize her story is mine. I am the ordinary girl. I truly am just an ordinary girl, and I actually have experienced a lifetime full of extraordinary love. I knew my story needed to be told. I just could not write about myself in the first person!

As GG mentioned earlier, the idea for this book came long before I met her dad and found that love of a lover that we all seek. Tracy and I enjoyed many years as empty nesters before we adopted GG. Then as I watched her grow and mature, an idea came to me: I was going to have *her* tell *my* story.

When Tracy chose to end his cancer treatment and started hospice care, he continued to beg me to write. One of my last gifts to him was finally starting the book. Tracy read and blessed the outline and shared with me many of his memories of our love story before he died.

The final chapter, "Love of Life," was originally going to be the summary of *my* life, and it was supposed to tie all the other chapters together. But when Tracy died, the book, as well as my life, took yet another winding turn, and the decision to write a chapter that was solely about him became the obvious choice.

I have been a teen mother, experienced the divorce of my parents and my own divorce, and lived through bankruptcy. I lived through the devastating, professional, and personal damage of a hurricane while caring for a dying husband who was also my business partner. I mourned the premature deaths of three younger brothers and a husband. During these traumatic life experiences, I was observing my own life, finding meaning in the chaos, appreciating the blessings, and ultimately figuring out who I am. I learned from hard times that I had to love myself and find the good in everyone and love the world around me before I could truly open my heart to love someone else. Once my heart was open to those other types of love, it was quite ready to recognize and nurture the love I have with and for Tracy. And while his death at such a young age shocked and saddened me, I am so much better. For the almost eighteen years that he was in my life, the pain was well worth experiencing. I truly believe the old adage that says, "It is better to have loved and lost than to never have loved at all."

I assert that the ability to be open to love—all kinds of love—is a chosen and learned experience and not necessarily a function of luck or even a feeling. I believe that genuine, extraordinary love is all around us, but we often have our eyes closed to it. I am blessed to have learned early in life that love surrounds me in spite of what circumstances are happening in my world; I just had to open my heart to it and acknowledge it. For example, I have not always been in a relationship, but I have always been surrounded by people who love me and whom I love. I have not always had money in the bank, but I always had food on the table. I have not always lived where I wanted, but I have always had love in my home and beautiful flowers to smell. The weather is not always sunny, but I have learned to find joy in even the worst storms. I believe that appreciating what one has is the first step to enjoying extraordinary love.

Speaking of storms, it rained cats and dogs on my and Tracy's wedding day. We planned to be married on the beach at sunrise and to kayak in the Gulf of Mexico, which would be our escape from the wedding reception, but it was raining so hard there was no way for that to happen without risking a call to the Coast Guard! Yet we had the most amazing wedding day in spite of it; it happened in a room full of love—the love of friends, family, God, and each other. It was a wonderful celebration! Rather than kayaking in the Gulf, we kayaked in the flooded parking lot and waved good-bye to all the people who were supposed to see us off as they left. So even though I had planned for a sunrise wedding on the beach, the storm of that day shifted the focus off the setting and the wedding and on to our hearts and our marriage. We ended up with some really fun memories as well. God's plan is always perfect.

Ironically, it also rained in the form of a hurricane when Tracy was receiving at-home hospice care and we were facing the end of our life together as a couple. Even though he had not eaten in weeks and was very weak and frail, we called that Harvey night a date night. After the power went out, I posted on Facebook a photo of candles illuminating what was left of our lives and entitled it *Just Another Ordinary Friday Night*. The last photo taken of him was snapped during that storm. We took an "us-ee (what our grandchildren call a selfie with more than one person)" by candlelight. It was horribly sad to experience the hurricane and his death during the same time frame, but I will never forget our last date and am grateful to have had our treasured time together.

I believe that by being grateful for all the experiences in my life and embracing the roller coaster that *is* life, I become more open to love. Learning to look for the good in the world helps me find the good that leads to extraordinary love. I have lived an extraordinary life and experienced extraordinary love. I continue to be open to more of it.

As we prepare to publish GG's story, we approach the second anniversaries of Hurricane Harvey and Tracy's death, which happened four weeks after the hurricane. Our entire world has changed. Our community is still rebuilding, and it will take time before it feels or looks normal. I too am rebuilding and figuring out who I am as a single woman who is living alone for the first time in her life. In spite of the challenges—or maybe because of them—I feel strong and happy. God has blessed me beyond measure, and I know that he will continue to hold my hand as GG and I explore the world without her dad.

The Bottom Line for Those Seeking Extraordinary Love

I hope you have found something in GG's story that will help you find your own extraordinary love. Remember to remain open to what happens in life. Accept the bad with the good, and *find* the good in all events. In the early pages of this memoir, GG encouraged you to write your own story and share it with us. I truly hope you will. You can send it to us via e-mail to ExtraordinaryWiseDog@ gmail.com, or find us on Facebook.

ABOUT THE AUTHOR

Tammie Homeyer Shelton is a business owner and author. She has lived in the Coastal Bend of Texas, near Corpus Christi, all her life. A voracious learner, she studies extensively and holds a certificate in education for ministry from the School of Theology of the University of the South via its extension program. She has also earned a bachelor of science degree and a master's degree in public administration from Texas A&M University—Corpus Christi. More importantly, she has learned from a sometimes-tragic and often-chaotic life and is grateful for her streetwise education. A lifelong Christian, she credits her faith in God and those life lessons for her ability to find happiness and joy no matter what circumstances surround her. She describes herself as an ordinary girl but recognizes that she has experienced an amazing life that is filled with extraordinary love. She enjoys her ministry of teaching people with disabilities how to scuba dive and escorting them on scuba vacations in the Caribbean. She is grateful for any time she manages to spend with her three grown children and their families, which include nine grandchildren. A self-proclaimed beach addict, she lives on the coast with her wise dog and coauthor, GG. They enjoy getting a saltwater fix and watching the sun rise or set over the water every day.